MW01615216

Take a trip down memory lane with this look back at 1975. The fall of Saigon takes place, Jimmy Hoffa disappears, the Khmer Rouge regime takes over Cambodia, the U.S. and Russia meet in space, Microsoft is founded, New York City narrowly avoids bankruptcy and the SS *Edmund Fitzgerald* sinks in the icy waters of Lake Superior. Remember the stories, photos, news, people, advertisements, sports and events that made 1975 your special year!

A walk back in time...

To:

From:

Managing Editor • Art Worthington

Publishers • Lawrence Siegel & Art Worthington

Cover Design • Peter Hess

Designer • Liz Howard

Writing & Research • Liz Howard

Facilitator • Pamela Thomas

.com

(800) 541-3533

1975 Music Scene

NT EASTWOOD

HIS LIFELINE –
held by the assassin
he hunted.

EIGER SANCTI
EORGE KENNEDY

THE ROCKY
HORROR
PICTURE SHOW

a different
set of jaws

STREISA

Funny Lady

BARBRA STREISAND and JAMES CAAN
FUNNY LADY
OMAR SHARIF

now
playing
at the

ha, Bobby and Rose • Attilas '74 • The Apple
• The Black Bird • Breakheart Pass • Breakout
sino of Gold • Cooley High • Coonskin • Conduct
y Afternoon • The Drowning Pool • The Eiger
• The Flower in His Mouth • The Fortune • The
aldo Pepper • The Happy Hooker • Hard Times
My Father Told Me • The Man in the Glass Booth
Monty Python and the Holy Grail • Moonrunners
er Side of the Mountain • Overlord • Race with
Reincarnation of Peter Proud • The Return of the
r Cogburn • Royal Flash • Shampoo • Smile
Tommy • Ultimate Warrior • W.W. and the Dixie
he Wind and the Lion • A Woman's Decision

MOVIES

Why Detroit's engineers are secretly praising Volkswagen's Rabbit.

Happy days are here again.

One thing about the men of the engineering profession: they give credit where credit is due. Which may explain all the nice letters and phone calls we've received from Detroit since our new Rabbit has been out. Why all the praise?

93 miles per hour.

A Rabbit is very fast. And although we obviously don't recommend 93 mph (please obey all speed limits), it is reassuring to know as you're about to get onto a hectic expressway, that a Rabbit has the power for great acceleration. From 0 to 50 in only 8.2 seconds. That's quicker than a Monza 2 + 2.

38 miles per gallon.

A Rabbit is very thrifty. In the recent 1975-model Federal Environmental Protection Agency fuel economy tests, the Rabbit averaged 38 miles to the gallon on the highway. It averaged a nifty 24 in tougher stop-and-go city traffic.

As big inside as some mid-size cars.

The Rabbit is a sub-compact sized car. That's on the outside. Open the door and it's a different story. 80% of the space in the car is devoted to functional room. There's actually more head and leg room inside than in some mid-size cars.

You get this feeling of roominess immediately, as you stretch out behind the wheel and look out through the huge front windshield. Visibility is incredible.

The main engineering feat that makes all this room possible is our revolutionary transverse engine, or stated more simply, an engine that is mounted sideways. Besides adding space, placing the engine in this manner, and slanting it, has a lot to do with why the Rabbit gets such good gas mileage. For now you have a very low silhouetted front end which means lower wind resistance, which means better gas mileage.

The Rabbit comes only one way, as a Hatchback. And you don't pay a penny more for that extra door. In addition to the 2-door model shown, there is a 4-door available. Four doors plus a Hatchback. That's a lot of ins and outs in one car.

How we got it to handle so easily.

The best way to describe driving a Rabbit is that it just feels right. The rack-and-pinion steering, designed exclusively for the Rabbit, allows you to feel in complete control, especially on fast, tight turns.

Another VW exclusive, an independent stabilizer rear axle, means independent wheel travel far more riding comfort and added safety on rough roads.

As is true on only two Detroit cars, the Eldorado and Toronado, the Rabbit has front-wheel drive for road-hugging ability. The firm and sporty ride of the car is enhanced by rigid unitized body/chassis construction, controlled spring and shock rates and longer suspension travel.

Owner's Security Blanket.

To make sure your Rabbit lives a lively and a carefree life, it's backed by the most advanced car coverage plan in the automotive industry: The Volkswagen Owner's Security Blanket with exclusive Computer Analysis.[1]

All for $2,999.*

Lately, a lot of automotive executives have been giving speeches on "the car of the future." They see it as being small, low-priced, but with increased interior dimensions and more economical performance.

Ladies and gentlemen of the automotive industry, your car of the future, our Rabbit, is here today.

And it will only cost you $2,999 to try it out. Happy days are here again.

rabbit

TOP GROSSING FILMS OF 1975

1. *Jaws* $260,000,000
2. *The Rocky Horror Picture Show* . . $112,892,319*
3. *One Flew Over the Cuckoo's Nest* . . $108,981,275
4. *Dog Day Afternoon* $50,000,000
5. *Shampoo* $49,407,734
6. *Tommy* $20,170,000
7. *Three Days of the Condor* $20,014,000
8. *Funny Lady* $19,313,000
9. *Nashville* $18,012,000
10. *The Day of the Locust* $17,793,000

* After theatrical re-issues (film is still in limited release as a cult classic).

Oscars® Presented in 1975
for 1974 films

Best Picture
The Godfather: Part II

Best Director
Francis Ford Coppola,
The Godfather: Part II

Best Actor
Art Carney, Harry and Tonto

Best Actress
Ellen Burstyn,
Alice Doesn't Live Here Anymore

Best Supporting Actor
Robert De Niro,
The Godfather: Part II

Best Supporting Actress
Ingrid Bergman,
Murder on the Orient Express

Best Song
"We May Never Love Like This Again,"
The Towering Inferno

Oscars® Presented in 1976
for 1975 films

Best Picture
One Flew Over the Cuckoo's Nest

Best Director
Miloš Forman, One Flew Over the
Cuckoo's Nest

Best Actor
Jack Nicholson, One Flew
Over the Cuckoo's Nest

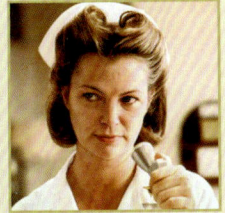

Best Actress
Louise Fletcher,
One Flew Over the
Cuckoo's Nest

Best Supporting Actor
George Burns,
The Sunshine Boys

Best Supporting Actress
Lee Grant, Shampoo

Best Song
"I'm Easy," Nashville

TELEV

TOP TWENTY

1. All in the Family
2. Sanford and Son
3. Chico and the Man
4. The Jeffersons
5. M*A*S*H
6. Rhoda
7. Good Times
8. The Waltons
9. Maude
10. Hawaii Five-O
11. The Mary Tyler Moore Show
12. The Rockford Files
13. Little House on the Prairie
14. Kojak
15. Police Woman
16. S.W.A.T.
17. The Bob Newhart Show
18. The Wonderful World of Disney
19. The Rookies
20. Mannix

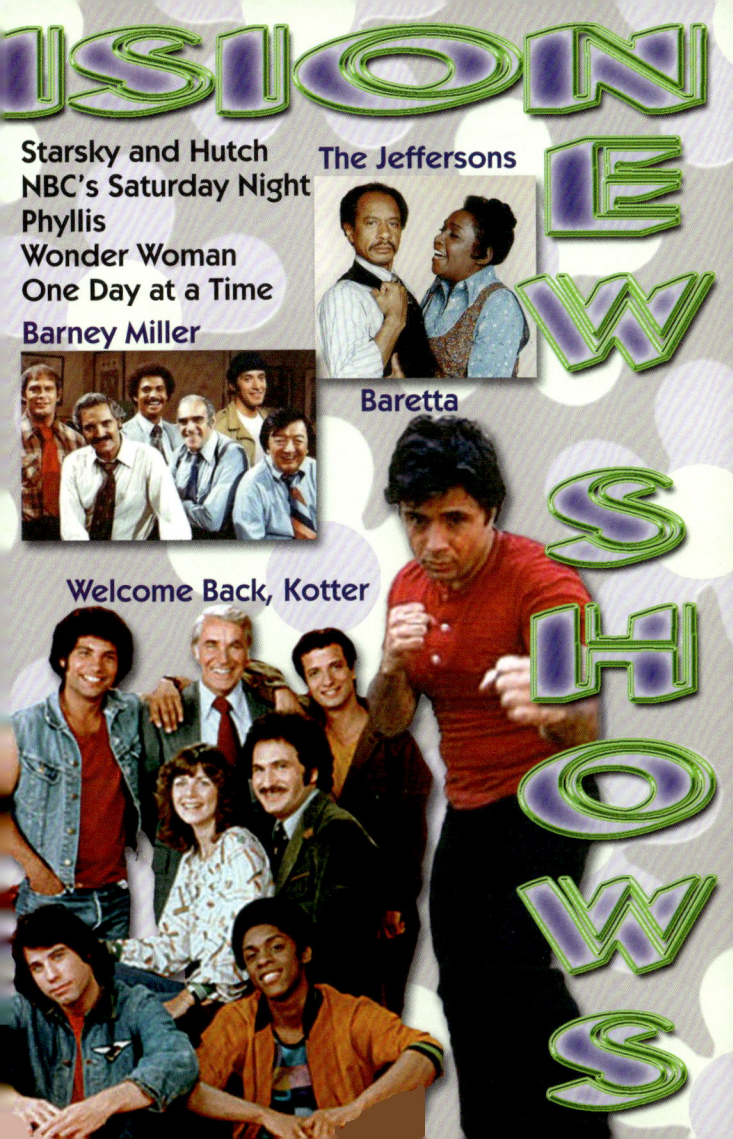

ISION

EW S

S HOWS

Starsky and Hutch
NBC's Saturday Night
Phyllis
Wonder Woman
One Day at a Time
Barney Miller

The Jeffersons

Baretta

Welcome Back, Kotter

NBC'S Saturday Night

The "Not Ready for Prime Time Players" change the face of late night television when NBC's Saturday Night (the name changes to Saturday Night Live in 1977) hits the air in October. The cast consists of Dan Aykroyd, John Belushi, Chevy Chase, Jane Curtin, Laraine Newman, Garrett Morris and Gilda Radner with a different guest host and musical act each week. Soon the focus shifts away from the hosts and music and onto the sketch comedy, with skits like the killer bees and land shark.

PRIME TIME LINEUP
1975–76 Fall Schedule

		7:00	7:30	8:00	8:30	9:00	9:30	10:00	10:30
SUNDAY	ABC	The Swiss Family Robinson		The Six Million Dollar Man		ABC Sunday Night Movie			
	CBS	Three for the Road		Cher		Kojak		Bronk	
	NBC	The Wonderful World of Disney		The Family Holvak		NBC Sunday Mystery Movie: Columbo/ McCloud/MacMillian and Wife/McCoy			
MONDAY	ABC	Local	Local	Barbary Coast		ABC Monday Night Football			
	CBS	Local	Local	Rhoda	Phyllis	All in the Family	Maude	Medical Center	
	NBC	Local	Local	The Invisible Man		NBC Monday Night at the Movies			
TUESDAY	ABC	Local	Local	Happy Days	Welcome Back, Kotter	The Rookies		Marcus Welby, M.D.	
	CBS	Local	Local	Good Times	Joe and Sons	Switch		Beacon Hill	
	NBC	Local	Local	Movin' On		Police Story		Joe Forrester	
WEDNESDAY	ABC	Local	Local	When Things Were Rotten	That's My Mama	Baretta		Starsky and Hutch	
	CBS	Local	Local	Tony Orlando and Dawn		Cannon		Kate McShane	
	NBC	Local	Local	Little House on the Prairie		Doctors' Hospital		Petrocelli	
THURSDAY	ABC	Local	Local	Barney Miller	On the Rocks	The Streets of San Francisco		Harry O	
	CBS	Local	Local	The Waltons		CBS Thursday Night Movie			
	NBC	Local	Local	The Montefuscos	Fay	Ellery Queen		Medical Story	
FRIDAY	ABC	Local	Local	Mobile One		The ABC Friday Night Movie			
	CBS	Local	Local	Big Eddie	M*A*S*H	Hawaii Five-O		Barnaby Jones	
	NBC	Local	Local	Sanford & Son	Chico and the Man	The Rockford Files		Police Woman	
SATURDAY	ABC	Local	Local	Saturday Night Live with Howard Cosell		S.W.A.T.		Matt Helm	
	CBS	Local	Local	The Jeffersons	Doc	The Mary Tyler Moore Show	The Bob Newhart Show	The Carol Burnett Show	
	NBC	Local	Local	Emergency		NBC Saturday Night Movie			

ON THE RADIO

Best of My Love - Eagles; Black Friday - Steely Dan; Black Water - The Doobie Brothers; Bohemian Rhapsody - Queen; Born to Run - Bruce Springsteen; The Boys Are Back in Town - Thin Lizzy; Convoy - C. W. McCall; Dreamer - Supertramp; Feel Like Makin' Love - Bad Company; Fox on the Run - Sweet; Get Down Tonight - KC and the Sunshine Band; Golden Years - David Bowie; Good Lovin' Gone Bad - Bad Company; Have a Cigar - Pink Floyd; Have You Never Been Mellow - Olivia Newton-John; He Don't Love You (Like I Love You) - Tony Orlando and Dawn; High Voltage - AC/DC; The Hustle - Van McCoy; I Write the Songs - Barry Manilow; I'm Not in Love - 10cc; Island Girl - Elton John; It's a Long Way to the Top - AC/DC; Knockin' on Heaven's Door - Eric Clapton; Kung Fu Fighting - Carl Douglas; Lady - Styx; Laughter in the Rain - Neil Sedaka; Lonely People - America; Love Hurts - Jim Capaldi; Love to Love You Baby - Donna Summer; Love Will Keep Us Together - Captain & Tennille; Low Rider - War; Lucy in the Sky with Diamonds - Elton John; Lyin' Eyes - Eagles; Magic - Pilot; Mandy - Barry Manilow; Miracles - Jefferson Starship; One of These Nights - Eagles; Only Women Bleed - Alice Cooper; Please Mr. Postman - The Carpenters; Rhinestone Cowboy - Glen Campbell; Rock and Roll All Nite - KISS; Roll on Down the Highway - Bachman-Turner Overdrive; Saturday Night - Bay City Rollers; Saturday Night Special - Lynyrd Skynyrd; Sister Golden Hair - America; Slow Ride - Foghat; Someone Saved My Life Tonight - Elton John; Space Oddity - David Bowie; Spirit in the Night - Manfred Mann's Earth Band; Squeeze Box - The Who; Strange Magic - Electric Light Orchestra; SOS - ABBA; Sweet Emotion - Aerosmith; Thank God I'm a Country Boy - John Denver; That's the Way (I Like It) - KC and the Sunshine Band; You Are So Beautiful - Joe Cocker; You Sexy Thing - Hot Chocolate; Young Americans - David Bowie; You're My Best Friend - Queen; You're No Good - Linda Ronstadt; Walk This Way - Aerosmith; Wasted Days and Wasted Nights - Freddy Fender; Welcome to the Machine - Pink Floyd; When Will I Be Loved - Linda Ronstadt; Why Can't We Be Friends - War

Music

The Outlaws release their debut album, *Outlaws*, which contains the nearly 10-minute song, *Green Grass & High Tides*.

Born to Run, the third album by Bruce Springsteen, is released. It is Springsteen's breakthrough album, peaking at number 3 on the Billboard charts and is considered by many to be one of the greatest rock albums of all time. Two of the tracks, *Born to Run* and *Thunder Road*, are number 21 and 86 respectively on *Rolling Stone* magazine's list of the 500 Greatest Songs of All Time.

Patti Smith, a popular performer on the New York punk scene, release her first album, *Horses*.

Bob Marley and the Wailers release their album *Live!* which was recorded July 18th and 19th 1975 at the Lyceum Theatre in London. The album contains the hits *No Woman, No Cry, I Shot the Sheriff,* and *Get Up, Stand Up.*

Notes

Musician Steve Miller is arrested for setting fire to the clothes and possessions of a friend, and resisting arrest. The charges are dropped the next day.

This year Deborah Harry and guitarist Chris Stein form the band Angel and the Snake and begin playing the New York punk rock scene. Later in the year they change the name of the band to Blondie.

BILLBOARD TOP 10 U.S. HITS FOR 1975

Love Will Keep Us Together, Captain & Tennille

Rhinestone Cowboy, Glen Campbell

Philadelphia Freedom, Elton John

Before the Next Teardrop Falls, Freddy Fender

My Eyes Adored You, Frankie Valli

Shining Star, Earth, Wind & Fire

Fame, David Bowie

Laughter in the Rain, Neil Sedaka

One of These Nights, Eagles

Thank God I'm a Country Boy, John Denver

Founding member of the group Badfinger Peter Ham commits suicide by hanging himself in his London garage.

Peter Gabriel leaves British rock group Genesis.

Linda McCartney is arrested for possession of marijuana when she and her husband, former Beatle Paul McCartney, are pulled over for a routine traffic stop in Los Angeles.

AWARDS

GRAMMY AWARDS

RECORD OF THE YEAR:
Love Will Keep Us Together, *Captain & Tennille*

ALBUM OF THE YEAR:
Still Crazy After All These Years, *Paul Simon*

SONG OF THE YEAR:
Send in the Clowns, *Stephen Sondheim, writer*

BEST NEW ARTIST:
Natalie Cole

BEST POP VOCAL:
MALE:
Paul Simon, *Still Crazy After All These Years*

FEMALE:
Janis Ian, *At Seventeen*

DUO, GROUP/CHORUS:
The Eagles, *Lyin' Eyes*

BEST R&B VOCAL:
MALE:
Ray Charles, *Living for the City*

FEMALE:
Natalie Cole, *This Will Be*

DUO, GROUP/CHORUS:
Earth, Wind & Fire, *Shining Star*

Awarded in 1976.

PULITZER PRIZES

PUBLIC SERVICE:
The Boston Globe
For its massive and balanced coverage of the Boston school desegregation crisis.

FICTION:
Michael Shaara
The Killer Angels

DRAMA:
Edward Albee
Seascape

POETRY:
Gary Snyder
Turtle Island

HISTORY:
Dumas Malone
Jefferson and His Time, Vols. I-V

BIOGRAPHY OR AUTOBIOGRAPHY:
Robert Caro
The Power Broker: Robert Moses and the Fall of New York

MUSIC:
Dominick Argento
From the Diary of Virginia Woolf

An earthquake in China is claimed by the Chinese government to have been successfully predicted, however it still kills 2,041 and injures 27,538 in Haicheng, Liaoning.

In September, a 6.7 magnitude earthquake kills over 2,000 people in Turkey.

A subway crash at Moorgate station in London kills 43 people.

A fire breaks out on the 11th floor of the World Trade Center's North Tower at 11:45 on the evening of February 13th and spreads through cable tunnels to the 9th and 19th floors. No one is killed in the intense blaze, but 28 fire-fighters are injured and over $2,000,000 in damage is sustained.

In China's Henan Province, Super Typhoon Nina and a cold front collide and the result is torrential rains, more than 3 feet in 3 days, causing a 1-in-2,000-year flood. On August 8th the immense amount of rain is too much for the Shimantan Dam on the Hong River. Just past midnight the water crests the dam and it fails, sending a wall of water downstream into the larger Banqiao reservoir. Just after 1 a.m. the Banqiao Dam is crested and it too fails. Now a 6.2-mile-wide wave between 9.8 and 23 feet tall rushes into the plains below at nearly 31 miles an hour, decimating a 34-mile long, 9.3-mile wide area with little or no warning. Some 60 other dams fail as a result of the first two and 4,600 square miles which includes seven county seats and numerous communities are under water. An estimated 11 million residents in the area are affected, close to 6 million buildings are destroyed, and the loss of life is an astounding 26,000 from the flooding and another 145,000 due to subsequent epidemics and famine.

A bomb planted at the baggage claim area at New York's LaGuardia Airport on December 29 explodes, killing 14 people and injuring 70 others.

DISASTERS

The first flight of Operation Babylift, a U.S. mission to get Vietnamese orphans out of the Vietnam before the fall of Saigon, experiences serious trouble 12 minutes after takeoff and tries to make an emergency landing. The C-5A Galaxy's cargo door locks failed, ripping open the door and severing the control cables to the tail, causing two of four hydraulic systems to fail. Despite the flight crew's valiant efforts to land the compromised plane at Tan Son Nhut Air Base, the plane crashes in a rice paddy, breaking into four pieces and killing 153, of the 328 people on board. 76 orphaned children are killed.

On final approach to New York's JFK International Airport, Eastern Air Lines Flight 66 from New Orleans encounters a wind shear and begins clipping the approach lights 2,400 feet before the start of the runway. The plane continues striking the lights until it bursts into flames, killing 113 of the 124 people on board.

In heavy fog a charter Boeing 707 carrying Moroccan immigrant workers home from France smashes a mountainside just minutes before it is due to land at the Agadir airport. All 188 people on board are killed.

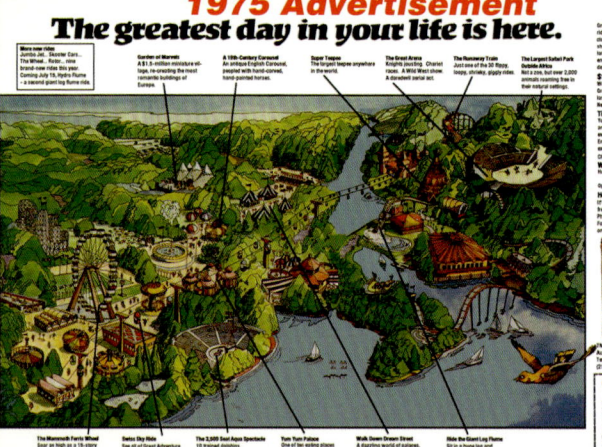

July 17 and 18th bring the worst frost in a century to Brazil destroying 1.5 billion coffee trees, more than half the trees in the nation. Although most of the harvest is complete, other coffee-producing nations halt exports hoping for higher prices. Within two weeks of the frost the price of retail coffee is up 20 cents per pound.

The SS *Edmund Fitzgerald*, one of the largest iron ore freighters on the Great Lakes, sinks November 10th during a fierce gale 17 miles short of Whitefish Bay on Lake Superior. On the 9th the *Fitzgerald* leaves Superior, Wisconsin fully loaded heading for steel mills near Detroit, Michigan and is joined by another freighter, the SS *Arthur M. Anderson* heading to Gary, Indiana. With the *Fitzgerald* in the lead they head out across Superior, soon encountering a severe winter storm. The gale rages through the night with waves up to 35 feet high and winds in excess of 58 miles per hour. In the late afternoon on the 10th *Fitzgerald* radios *Anderson* reporting a minor list and top-side damage causing the loss of their radar. Visibility is poor due to heavy snow so *Fitzgerald* slows and *Anderson* comes within 10 miles giving her radar guidance. Shortly thereafter the Coast Guard advises all ships seek safe harbor and *Anderson* directs *Fitzgerald* toward Whitefish Bay and the safety it offers. By 5:45 *Fitzgerald*'s list has become serious and heavy seas are washing across her decks. At 7:10 *Anderson* and *Fitzgerald* have their final communication, with *Fitzgerald*'s captain reporting "We are holding our own." Just moments later *Fitzgerald* disappears from radar with no distress call, sinking in just moments in 50 feet of water. Her entire crew of 29 perish, no bodies are recovered and the exact cause of the wreck remains debatable. The disaster is immortalized in Gordon Lightfoot's 1976 hit *The Wreck of the Edmund Fitzgerald*.

DISASTERS

1975 Advertisement

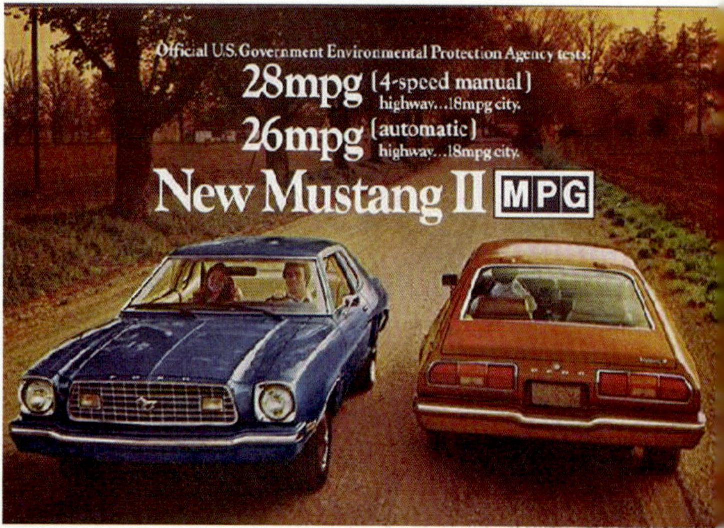

Left, Mustang II MPG Hardtop • Right, Mustang II MPG 2+2

Better mileage than any small luxury car. Lower priced than any foreign competitor.

MPG This insignia tells you California's best-selling small luxury car now gives you the luxury of increased mileage. Official EPA highway tests got 28 miles to a gallon (18 mpg city) with a 4-speed manual transmission. Even with automatic transmission, the new Mustang II MPG got better mileage than many imports. Along with good mileage you get the standard Mustang II equipment: tachometer, rack and pinion steering, steel-belted radials, floor-mounted 4-speed stick—and the same low Mustang II price. Order now for quick delivery.

Mustang II MPG Ghia. Opera windows, vinyl roof and bodyside moldings are just some of the elegant touches that are standard on Ghia and make it such a distinctive small luxury car.

Mustang II MPG $3,529*

$2,534 less than Datsun 280Z
$175 less than Toyota Celica ST
$718 less than VW Dasher
$1,157 less than VW Scirocco
$855 less than Mazda RX4

And $320 less than Monza Towne Coupe with its 5-speed option, which is required to achieve its best mileage results.

MPG equipment:
Mustang II MPG equipped with 2.3-liter 2V 4-cylinder engine, 4-speed manual (or optional automatic) transmission, a 3.40 axle ratio and catalytic converter.

*Base sticker price of Mustang II MPG Hardtop excluding title, taxes, destination ($230), required California equipment ($41) and dealer prep. Price comparisons based on sticker prices. Because dealer prep is extra on all cars except GM and Toyota cars, the price difference may vary in some areas.

Ford makes cars trucks and jobs in California.

FORD

FORD DIVISION

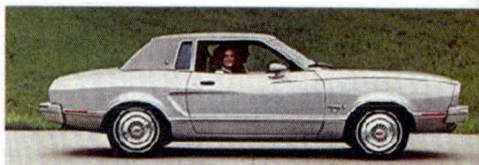

WORLD

AFRICA: Some 350,000 unarmed Moroccans cross the border into the Western Sahara in hopes of forcing Spain to hand over the Spanish Province of Sahara to Morocco. The Green March takes place in November as Franco lay dying, and in order to avoid war Spain agrees to negotiations with Morocco and brings Mauritania into the mix as well. The result is the November 14 Madrid Accords, a treaty dividing Spanish Sahara between Mauritania and Morocco.

The Treaty of Lagos is signed by 15 West African countries, instituting the Economic Community of West African States.

BANGLADESH: Sheikh Mujibur Rahman, Prime Minister of Bangladesh, declares a state of emergency in January. His supporters approve a constitutional amendment banning all opposing political parties and he becomes president. In August a coup lead by his colleague and former confidante Khondaker Mostaq Ahmad leads to the assassination of Mujibur and most of his family. Ahmad takes office and years of political turmoil follow.

BRAZIL: The state of Guanabara merges with the state of Rio de Janeiro and becomes Rio de Janeiro. The state's capital is moved from Niterói to the city of Rio de Janeiro.

EVENTS

WORLD

ENGLAND: Margaret Thatcher is elected as the first female leader of the British Conservative Party.

In November, Iceland declares that the ocean up to 200 nautical miles from its coast belongs to Iceland and the Third Cod War between England and Iceland ensues.

The inflation rate jumps to 25% and unemployment reaches 1.25 million. Prime Minister Harold Wilson states that the government needs to focus on aiding industrial development and rejuvenation rather than programs such as nationalized health care and subsidized housing.

The Sex Discrimination Act and the Equal Pay Act come into effect in November. The law requires women to receive equal pay to that of men in the same line of work, giving employers five years to upgrade women's wages.

The PIRA bombs a Hilton Hotel in London on September 5th; 2 people are killed and 63 are injured.

Ross McWhirter, co-founder of the Guinness Book of Records, is killed by IRA members.

INDIA: India's first female prime minister, Indira Gandhi, is found guilty of violating election laws and although there are calls for her resignation, she refuses and orders the arrests of more than 750 of her opponents. Civil unrest, protests and rioting ensue

EVENTS

in New Delhi, and Gandhi declares a state of emergency in India and proceeds to grant herself extraordinary powers effectively allowing her to rule by decree.

MIDDLE EAST: OPEC raises oil prices 10%.

King Faisal of Saudi Arabia is assassinated by his nephew who is in turn beheaded. King Khalid succeeds Faisal.

Iran and Iraq sign the Algiers Accord, a settlement of their border disputes. For the first time since the Six-Day War the Suez Canal is opened.

After five years of conflict between Lebanese and Palestinian refugees, Lebanon escalates into civil war as Christians take up arms against "Islamo-Progressivists." Although the PLO, headed by Yasir Arafat, agrees they will not involve themselves with Lebanon's affairs, Lebanon's President Suleiman Frangieh claims the PLO is violating the agreements and fueling the civil war. Radical Palestinian guerrillas invade an OPEC conference in late December, killing 3 and taking 81 members hostage, 11 of which are OPEC ministers. Some of the hostages are released over the next few days and the terrorists take the remaining hostages on a flight to Algeria. The last hostages are released in Algeria and the terrorists are guaranteed safe passage to Libya.

WORLD

SPAIN: Spanish dictator Francisco Franco dies in November and two days later Juan Carlos becomes King of Spain as decreed by Franco in 1969. The Spanish throne had been vacant for the past 22 years and Carlos successfully transitions Spain from a dictatorship to parliamentary democracy in the following years.

VIETNAM: On March 10th the North Vietnamese begin a major offensive against the South. The NVA marches toward Saigon capturing major cities of Hue on March 25th and Da Nang on the 28th, with more than 300,000 South Vietnamese refugees fleeing Da Nang. Although South Vietnam President Nguyen Van Thieu hopes for renewed American support none is forthcoming and the march continues, becoming known as the Ho Chi Minh campaign. On April 9th the last defense, the city of Xuan Loc, is reached and a last stand is made by the South who hold on until the 20th when the city is captured. The following day Thieu resigns on television and tearfully denounces the U.S. for not coming to their aid. By the 27th Saigon is surrounded and the fall of Saigon is inevitable. Following the destruction of Saigon's Tan Son Nhat airport on the morning of April 29th, Americans and friendly Vietnamese are instructed to report to pre-arranged

EVENTS

'74 R. J. Reynolds Tobacco Co.

If I'm going to smoke, I'm going to do it right.

Some people smoke a brand for its image.
I don't. You can't taste image. I smoke for taste.
I smoke Winston. All Winston will ever give you
is real taste. And real pleasure. For some of us,
that's enough. Winston is for real.

19 mg. "tar", 1.3 mg. nicotine av. per cigarette,
FTC Report OCT. '74.

New Toyota 5-speed Sport Truck.
And new is a word we don't use lightly.

SR-5 Sport Truck.

5-speed overdrive transmission.

Hi-back bucket seats.

185 SR x 14 fat radial tires.

Well-appointed instrument panel.

It's just not our style to run a stripe down the side and then scream "new."

To start with, there are five good reasons why we call it a Sport Truck.

1st, 2nd, 3rd, 4th and 5th. The gears in the 5-speed overdrive transmission.

And that's mostly what sets our new SR-5 Sport Truck apart from other half-ton trucks.

But keep reading. Because it goes on with personality.

It comes with Hi-back bucket seats, AM radio, thick pile carpeting and fat radial tires—as well as racing stripes.

In front of all that is our powerful new 2.2 liter hemi-head engine.

There's one more thing about the rugged new SR-5 Sport Truck.

It's designed and built with great deal of care.

But then you expect that kind of craftsmanship from Toyota.

Small car specialists for over 40 years

TOYOTA

See how much truck your money can buy.

VIETNAM *(continued)*: points and helicopter evacuations begin in earnest. At 3:45 a.m. on April 30th the evacuation efforts are refocused and only Americans are allowed to board the helicopters. The final helicopter leaves the American Embassy just before 8:00 a.m. on the 30th carrying the last American soldiers who had been guarding the embassy. At 10:45 a.m. the gates of the Independence Palace are bulldozed by the North Vietnamese and General Duong Van Minh, who had become president just two days prior, is arrested. At 3:30 in the afternoon Minh gives a radio broadcast stating that the South Vietnamese government has been completely dissolved and the Vietnam War is over. Saigon is renamed Ho Chi Minh City after the former president of North Vietnam and a victory celebration is held on May 7th.

Over 3,300 orphans are rescued from Vietnam in April thanks to America's Operation Babylift.

CAMBODIA: In April the horrific Khmer Rouge regime, led by Pol Pot, takes power in Cambodia. Pol Pot's goal of cleansing the country and restarting civilization to the year zero causes the deaths of an estimated 1.7 to 2.5 million people by the year 1979, when the Khmer Rouge government ends.

1975 Advertisement

IMAGES FROM THE FALL OF SAIGON

Dave Frelsen's Datsun 710, B-Sedan winner at Road Atlanta

CHAMP

DATSUN 710

93

DATSUN

Beauty is a Beast!

The new Datsun 710 has a split personality.

This beautiful mid-sized Datsun that goes so far on a gallon of gas is a brawny beast in competition.

Two Datsun 710s, driven by Dave Frelsen and Dave Madison, won 1974 Sports Car Club of America Regional B-Sedan Championships. Then, last November, Dave Frelsen's 710 fought off four competing makes and edged Bob Sharp's Datsun 610 by .30 seconds to win the SCCA National Championship for B-Sedans at Road Atlanta.

You can't exceed 55 miles per hour without breaking the law. But it's good to know that the same Datsun engineering know-how and durability are built into the 710 you can buy

at your dealer. Minus a few necessary racing modifications.

A Triple Crown for Datsun!

Datsun winning has become a tradition. In the same SCCA National Championships, a Datsun B-210, driven by Don Devendorf, ran away with the C-Sedan race. (This is the sharp little economy champion that got 39 miles per gallon on the highway in the 1975 EPA tests!) Another triumph for Datsun at Road Atlanta was in the C-Production competition when Walt Maas' 260-Z aced out second place Logan Blackburn in another 260-Z by just 1.5 seconds.

Going back, Datsuns have competed successfully in racing for years. What does this mean to you? That the Datsun you buy has been

proved on the racetrack, making it an exceptional value and a great performer.

Walt Maas' 260-Z C-Production winner at Road Atlanta

Free! Competition parts catalog.

Shows just about every accessory you could want for your Datsun. Complete with prices. Just mail your name and address on a postcard to: Competition Parts Catalog, Datsun Competition Dept., Section MT, P.O. Box 191, Carson, CA 90247.

710 Wagon and 710 2-Door Sedan. Luggage rack is optional.

Datsun Saves

IN AMERICA

Three Watergate conspirators, John N. Mitchell, H. R. Haldeman and John D. Erlichman, are found guilty and sentenced to prison.

Unemployment reaches 9.2% and President Gerald Ford admits the U.S. is in a recession.

Doctors strike for the first time ever this March in New York City. Taking to the picket lines for four days they demand increased pay for interns and residents as well as better working hours.

Vice President Nelson Rockefeller is appointed in January by President Ford to head up a special commission looking into alleged CIA domestic abuses. In June the Rockefeller Commission recommends a joint congressional oversight committee on intelligence.

Daylight savings time starts almost two months early in response to the energy crisis.

California Governor Ronald Reagan throws his hat in the ring for the Republican presidential nomination, challenging incumbent President Ford.

Congress votes to broaden the Voting Rights Act of 1965 to include Spanish-speaking Americans and other minorities with language barriers.

The Supreme Court reverses its 1961 ruling on all-male juries, and a Louisiana law that grants automatic exemption from jury duty to women violates the Sixth Amendment.

The Privacy Act of 1974 goes into effect September 27th, granting Americans the right to request, inspect and challenge their own federal files.

President Ford signs the Metric Conversion Act in December. Designed to move the U.S. toward adopting the metric system, compliance is voluntary and few Americans take the conversion seriously.

The Toxic Substances Control Act signed by President Ford requires cutting out production and sales of polychlorinated biphenyls (PCBs) within 3 years.

President Ford signs the Energy Policy and Conservation Act of 1975, setting gasoline mileage standards for cars and creating a Strategic Petroleum Reserve.

NEW YORK CITY FACES BANKRUPTCY

Washington plays hardball when it comes to New York City seeking a government handout to avoid bankruptcy. A compromise is reached and legislation is passed by the House of Representatives 275 to 130 December 15th and signed by President Ford on the 18th granting the city a loan of 2.3 billion each year until June 30, 1978—6.9 billion total. The loan must be repaid in the year it is made and comes with an interest rate 1% higher than the U.S. Treasury rate.

PRESIDENT Gerald Ford

Chase parodies Ford on NBC'S Saturday Night

Ford gains a reputation as a klutz when he has several mishaps. He falls on the steps of *Air Force One*, bumps his head entering *Marine One*, takes a spill while skiing and beans an onlooker in the head with a golf ball. The media has a field day with the blunders and comedian Chevy Chase relentlessly portrays Ford as a bumbling nincompoop on the new late night hit show *NBC'S Saturday Night*, driving the image of a clumsy president into America's consciousness.

On the serious side, two attempts on Ford's life are made just 17 days apart, both in California. September 5th, Charles Manson follower Lynette "Squeaky" Fromme points a gun at Ford in Sacramento. Fromme spends 34 years in jail.

In San Francisco Sara Jane Moore fires a shot at Ford and just misses him thanks to the quick reactions of a bystander, ex-marine Oliver Sipple, who pulls her arm down just as the shot is fired. Moore spends the next 32 years in jail.

Fromme

Moore

PEOPLE *in the* NEWS

Pine Ridge Indian Reservation, the scene of a 1973 American Indian Movement occupation, is again in the national spotlight when two young FBI agents are brutally murdered for no apparent reason. Agents **Ronald Williams** and **Jack Coler** are sent to arrest three residents of the reservation for allegedly kidnapping two people the day before. They are attacked with guns while still in their car and although they manage to call for help and turn the car around they fail to escape their assailants. They are dragged from the vehicle, stripped of their possessions and shot execution style. Several hours of gunfire between FBI agents and Indians ensue, one attacker is killed and 16 others injured.

Confederate General **Robert E. Lee** is granted a posthumous pardon by U.S. President **Ford**, and Lee's full rights of citizenship are restored.

Teamsters Union president **Jimmy Hoffa** is reported missing July 13th in Detroit, Michigan.

The Nobel Peace Prize is awarded to **Andrei D. Sakharov** of the USSR.

The first American Roman Catholic saint, **Elizabeth Seton**, is canonized September 14th.

Kidnapped newspaper heiress **Patricia Hearst** is placed on the FBI's Ten Most Wanted List after aligning herself with her kidnappers, the Symbionese Liberation Army. In September Hearst is arrested and convicted of bank robbery.

After drinking alcohol mixed with small doses of Librium and Valium 21-year-old **Karen Ann Quinlan** goes into coma. Quinlan is kept alive in a vegetative state on a ventilator and after several months her parents request that the hospital allow her to die. The hospital refuses and legal battles begin. A tribunal rules in her parents' favor and in 1976 she is taken off the ventilator. Quinlan continued to live in a persistent vegetative state for nearly another decade before dying from pneumonia.

Deaths this year:
**Susan Hayward
Ozzie Nelson
Aristotle Onassis
Rod Serling**

Some Firsts From 1975

* The first Bic disposable razor hits store shelves.

* Sony Betamax and JVC VHS are introduced.

* In New London, Connecticut the U.S. Coast Guard Academy admits women for the first time.

* Lever Brothers introduces their new toothpaste, Aim.

* The personal computer revolution starts when Micro Instrumentation and Telemetry Systems (MITS) of Albuquerque, New Mexico begins selling the microcomputer Altair 8800 do-it-yourself kit and an assembled version through mail order. Swamped with orders for the $400 machine the company is soon shipping more than 2,000 units per month. MITS founder Ed Roberts, soon begins working with a couple of programmers, Paul Allen and his childhood friend, Bill Gates, to develop a BASIC language for Roberts' computer.

* Microsoft is founded in Albuquerque, New Mexico by Bill Gates. Gates uses the term "mirco-soft" for the first time this year in a letter to Paul Allen, and trademarks it in 1976.

* On May 16th Japanese mountain climber Junko Tabei becomes the first woman to summit Mount Everest.

* Volkswagen begins selling the Golf in the U.S.

* The first programmable microwave, the Amana Touchmatic Radarange, hits the marketplace.

* In the U.S. soft drinks surpass coffee in popularity for the first time; next year they will pass milk.

* Giorgio Armani begins producing men's clothing in Milan.

* Ermal C. Fraze of Dayton, Ohio patents a new way to open aluminum cans that does away with the left-over pull tab.

Born in 1975

Zach Braff

Tiger Woods

Charlize Theron

Angelina Jolie

Kate Gosselin

Alicia Witt

Eva Longoria

Drew Barrymore

David Beckham

Tobey Maguire

Casey Affleck

Alex Rodriguez

1975 Magazine Cover

HOW TO "READ" FM TUNER SPECIFICATIONS

Popular Electronics

WORLD'S LARGEST-SELLING ELECTRONICS MAGAZINE   JANUARY 1975/75¢

PROJECT BREAKTHROUGH!

World's First Minicomputer Kit
to Rival Commercial Models...
"ALTAIR 8800"   SAVE OVER $1000

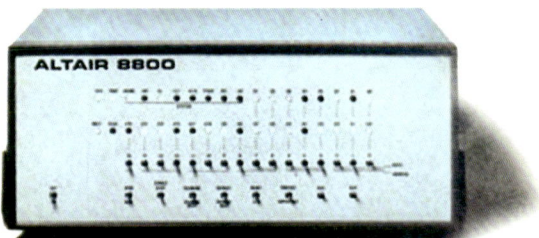

ALSO IN THIS ISSUE:

- An Under-$90 Scientific Calculator Project
  - CCD's—TV Camera Tube Successor?
  - Thyristor-Controlled Photoflashers

TEST REPORTS:

Technics 200 Speaker System
Pioneer RT-1011 Open-Reel Recorder
Tram Diamond-40 CB AM Transceiver
Edmund Scientific "Kirlian" Photo Kit
Hewlett-Packard 5381 Frequency Counter

18101

Determination has its rewards.

A tradition of building great cars like the 1933 Cadillac 355 Phaeton has its advantages—and rewards—for today's luxury car buyer. First, we stubbornly maintain that a luxury car should be a thing of beauty. This is reflected in all nine Cadillacs—including Eldorado, the only American-built luxury convertible. Then, there's Total Cadillac Value. Because of it, Cadillac resale is traditionally the highest of any U.S. luxury car make...and its repeat ownership the greatest of any U.S. car make. Cadillac. **Then and Now...an American Standard for the World.**

Cadillac '75

GM

MARK OF EXCELLENCE
Cadillac Motor Car Division

SCIENCE

NASA launches the *Viking 1* planetary probe headed for Mars.

The first joint U.S./Soviet space mission takes place with the Apollo-Soyuz Test Project. The American crew consists of Thomas Stafford, Vance Brand and one of the original Mercury Seven, Donald K. Slayton, on his first space flight. The Apollo crew docks with the Soviet *Soyus 19* and its crew Alexei Leonov and Valeri Kubasov in space on July 17th. Although the mission includes both joint and separate scientific experiments, it is the momentous international handshake that occurs in space, marking the end of the space race, that distinguishes the mission.

The U.K. begins pumping oil from the Brent Oilfield in the North Sea.

The Trans-Alaska pipeline construction begins when the first section of pipe is laid in the Tonsina River on March 27th. The 800-mile pipeline will be completed in May, 1977.

The Overthrust Belt, a 2,300-mile geological formation running from Alaska to Mexico through Canada, Idaho, Wyoming, Utah, Colorado and Arizona, has long been thought to contain billions of barrels of oil and natural gas. Oil was discovered along the belt in Canada in the 1920s and since then some 500 wells have been drilled along the western U.S. Overthrust Belt but none have produced until this year when, just 40 miles east of Salt Lake City, American Quasar Petroleum has a major strike and their Pineview field begins producing oil.

Nobel Prizes

PHYSICS
"for showing that the atomic nucleus is asymmetrical"

Leo James Rainwater

Ben Roy Mottelson

Aage N. Bohr

CHEMISTRY
"for research on structure of biological molecules such as antibiotics and cholesterol"

John W. Cornforth

Vladimir Prelog

PHYSIOLOGY OR MEDICINE
"for work in interaction between tumor viruses and genetic material of the cell"

David Baltimore

Howard M. Temin

Renato Dulbecco

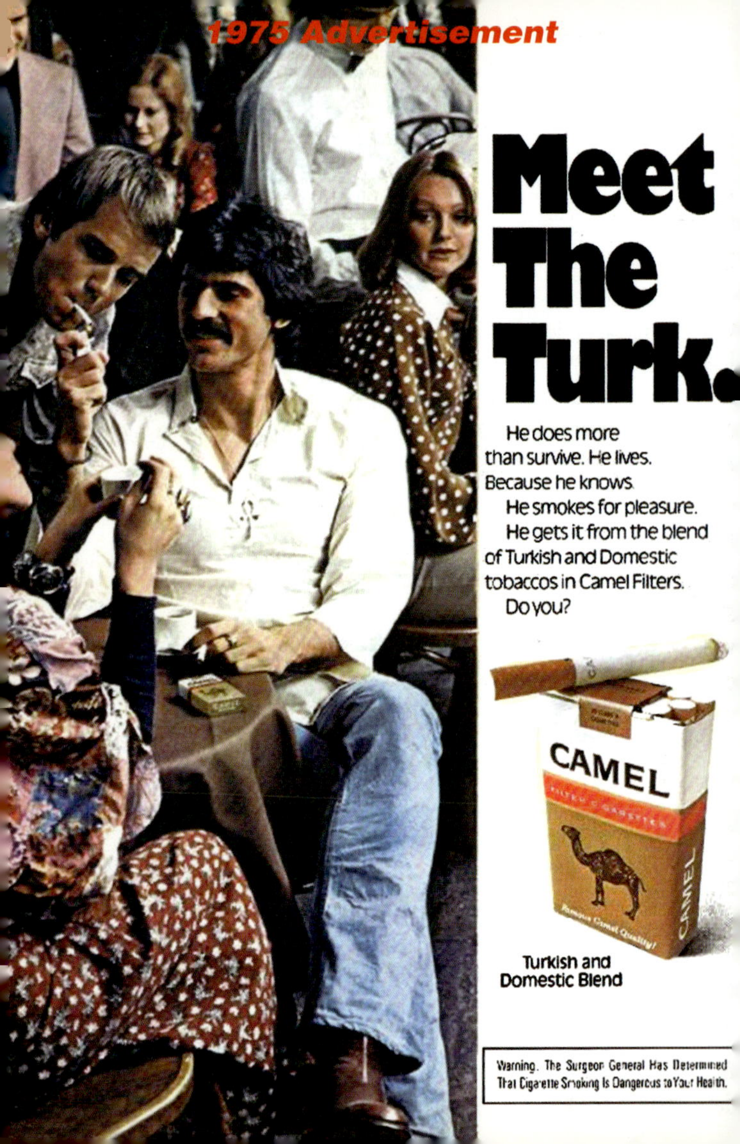
1975 Advertisement
Meet The Turk.
He does more than survive. He lives. Because he knows.
He smokes for pleasure.
He gets it from the blend of Turkish and Domestic tobaccos in Camel Filters.
Do you?
CAMEL
CAMEL
Turkish and Domestic Blend
Warning: The Surgeon General Has Determined That Cigarette Smoking Is Dangerous to Your Health.

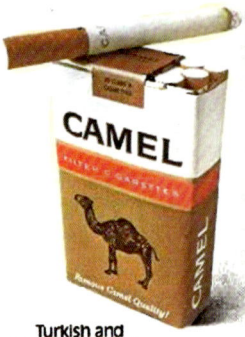

MEDICAL

Lyme disease is identified this year in Lyme, Connecticut. It is found to be transmitted to humans by a bite from a tick previously on deer, field mice and other animals. Left untreated it can cause serious problems with joints, heart, and central nervous system. Lyme disease quickly spreads throughout portions of the northeastern, mid-Atlantic, northern and western U.S.

Trying to staunch the flow of marijuana across the U.S./Mexico border a program funded by the U.S. begins spraying Mexican marijuana fields with a broad-leaf weed herbicide called paraquat. The marijuana is harvested and sold after being sprayed causing the CDC to issue warnings that smoking cannabis tainted with paraquat could cause serious lung damage. Despite the fact that no cases of poisoning are ever reported the U.S. government cuts off funding for the project in 1979 in response to marijuana smokers' demonstrations in Washington, D.C.

A nuclear-powered artificial heart is developed by Dr. Willem Kolff.

It is found that only 20 percent of the 725,000 hysterectomies that take place in the U.S. each year are treatment for cancer or life-threatening illnesses. The U.S. rate of hyster-ectomies is two and a half times greater than Britain and four times that of Sweden. U.S. hysterectomies have increased 25 percent in the past five years and there are more performed each year than there are tonsillectomies.

Immunologists Niels K. Jerne, César Milstein and Georges J. F. Köhler, develop a technique to produce monoclonal antibodies at the Laboratory of Molecular Biology in Cambridge, England.

The Federal Trade Commission launches an antitrust suit against the American Medical Association's ban on physician advertising. The FTC contends that by disallowing physician advertising it discourages competition and unfairly disadvantages consumers. The legal wrangling goes on for years but the FTC prevails and in 1982 the AMA's ban is lifted.

Just the Facts

UNITED STATES STATISTICS

Average Cost of a New House	$39,300.00
Average Income Per Year	14,100.00
Average Cost of a New Car	4,250.00
Average Monthly Rent	200.00
Minimum Hourly Wage	2.10
Cost of a Gallon of Gas	.44
Cost of a First-Class Stamp	.10
Consumer Price Index	53.8
Year-End Close Dow Jones Industrial Average	858
Unemployment	8.5%
Yearly Inflation Rate	9.2%
Interest Rates Year-End Federal Reserve	7.25%
Life Expectancy	72.6 years
Violent Crime Rate (per 1,000)	53.0
Property Crime Rate (per 1,000)	48.1

POPULATION

World	4,047,709,876
China	916,395,000
India	613,459,000
United States	215,973,000
Russia	134,200,000
Indonesia	132,589,000
Japan	111,940,000
Brazil	108,124,400
Germany	78,679,000
Bangladesh	73,178,170
Pakistan	71,033,000

Grocery Shopping

Lettuce (per head)	$ .25
Apples (3 lbs)	.59
Avocados	4 for 1.00
Red Grapes (per lb)	.25
Yellow Onion (per lb)	.15
Catsup (14 oz)	.37
Premium Soda Crackers	.59
Corn Flakes (12 oz)	.45
Hershey Bar (1.4 oz)	.15
Oreo Cookies (15 oz)	.89
Frozen Sausage Pizza (14 oz)	.89
Hawaiian Punch (quart)	1.69
Nestea Instant Mix (24 oz)	1.69
Strawberry Quik	1.69
Pepsi Cola (32 oz)	4 for 11.00
Jax Beer (12-oz 6 pack)	.99
Lonestar (12-oz 6 pack)	1.29
Old Milwaukee (12-oz 6 pack)	1.19
Paper Towels (jumbo roll)	.49
Johnson's Baby Shampoo	1.29
Herbal Essence Shampoo	1.19
Secret Spray-on Deodorant	2.25
Dove Bath Soap	3 for 1.00
Joy Liquid Detergent (22 oz)	.69
Cheer Laundry Soap (large)	1.15

Grocery Shopping

Bread	$ .69
Sugar (2-lb bag)	.69
Flour (25 lbs)	2.69
Butter (lb)	.99
Margarine (per lb)	.39
Eggs (dz grade A small)	.39
Milk (gal)	1.57
Turkey (per lb)	.65
Canned Ham (3 lbs)	5.99
T-Bone Steak (per lb)	.89
Rump Roast (per lb)	1.79
Hot Dogs (12-oz pkg)	.69
Short Ribs (per lb)	.79
Ground Beef (3 lbs)	1.19
Ground Chuck (per lb)	.89
Bacon (1 lb)	.99
Bologna (deli sliced per lb)	.89
Salami (deli sliced per lb)	.99
Potatoes (8 lbs)	.89
Rice (2 lbs)	.49
Green Beans (can)	3 for .89
Peas (can)	5 for 1.00
Corn (12-oz can)	4 for 1.00
Veg All (can)	3 for .89
Spinach (can)	.25

1975 Fashions

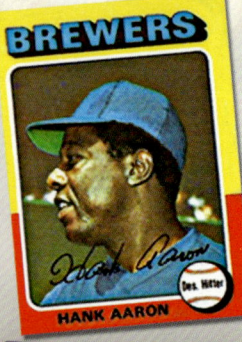

BREWERS

HANK AARON

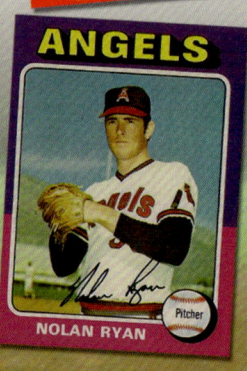

ANGELS

NOLAN RYAN · Pitcher

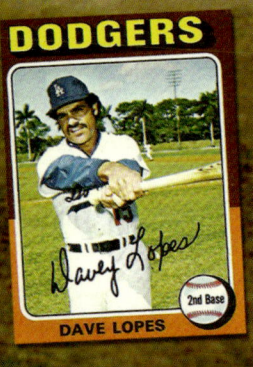

DODGERS

DAVE LOPES · 2nd Base

1975 MAJOR LEAGUE AWARDS

Most Valuable Player
Fred Lynn (AL)
Joe Morgan (NL)

Cy Young Award
Jim Palmer (AL)
Tom Seaver (NL)

Rookie of the Year
Fred Lynn (AL)
John Montefusco (NL)

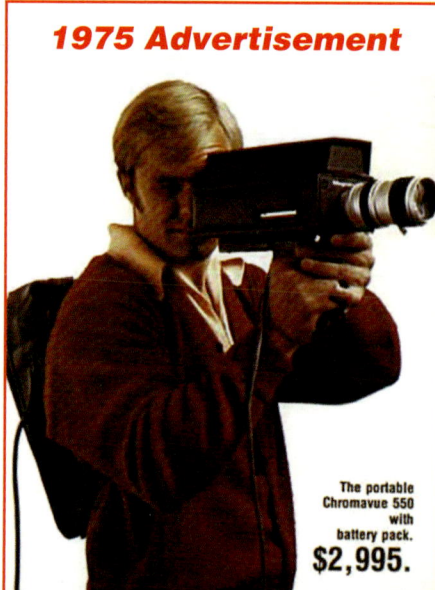

1975 Advertisement

The portable
Chromavue 550
with
battery pack.
$2,995.

In the American League Championship Series, the **Boston Red Sox** battle the **Oakland Athletics**, winning 3-0. Playing for the National League title the **Cincinnati Reds** take on the **Pittsburgh Pirates** beating them 3-0. The **Cincinnati Reds** face off against the **Boston Red Sox** for the World Series winning 4-3.

This year **Hank Aaron** breaks **Babe Ruth**'s RBI career total; **Nolan Ryan** ties **Sandy Koufax**'s record when he pitches his 4th career no-hitter; **Davey Lopes** steals his 32nd consecutive base without being caught, breaking the 1922 record set by **Max Carey**; and **Billy Martin** debuts as the New York Yankee's new manager.

World Series MVP
Pete Rose
Cincinnati Reds

BASEBALL

FOOTBALL

PRO BALL

This year marks the very first time referees are equipped with wireless microphones which allow them to announce penalties and clarify rulings for the fans and media.

The **Dallas Cowboys** defeat the **Minnesota Vikings** 17-14 in the Divisional Playoffs while the **Los Angeles Rams** defeat the **St. Louis Cardinals** 35-23, the **Oakland Raiders** defeat the **Cincinnati Bengals** 31-28; and the **Pittsburgh Steelers** take the **Baltimore Colts** 28-10. In the Conference Championships the **Cowboys** crush the **Rams** 37-7 and the **Steelers** beat the **Raiders** 16-10. The final showdown of the 1975 NFL season is played at **Super Bowl X** January 18, 1976 at the Miami Orange Bowl where it's the **Steelers** over the **Cowboys** 21-17, winning their second consecutive NFL Championship title.

COLLEGE BALL

The **University of Oklahoma Sooners** are the repeat national champions in the Associated Press writers' poll.

Orange Bowl
Oklahoma Sooners
over **Michigan Wolverines**
14-6

Cotton Bowl
Arkansas Razorbacks
over **Georgia Bulldogs**
31-10

Sugar Bowl
Alabama Crimson Tide
over **Penn State Nittany Lions**
13-6

Fiesta Bowl
Arizona State Sun Devils
over **Nebraska Cornhuskers**
17-14

Rose Bowl
UCLA Bruins
over **Ohio State Buckeyes**
23-10

Heisman Trophy
Archie Griffin
Ohio State

Vince Lombardi Award
Lee Roy Selmon
Oklahoma

All bowl games are played in January 1976.

PRO BALL

The Western Conference semifinals see the **Golden State Warriors** face the **Seattle SuperSonics**, winning 4-2, and the **Chicago Bulls** defeating the **Kansas City-Omaha Kings** 4-2. Meanwhile in the Eastern Conference the **Boston Celtics** beat the **Houston Rockets** 4-1, and the **Washington Bullets** defeat the **Buffalo Braves** 4-3. In the Conference finals the **Warriors** take the **Bulls** 4-3 and the **Bullets** beat the **Celtics** 4-2. The **Warriors** crush the Bullets 4-0 and are NBA World Champions.

COLLEGE BALL

In the Final Four **Kentucky** beats **Syracuse** 95-79 and **UCLA** beats **Louisville** 75-74. For their tenth and final NCAA Championship under the direction of coach **John Wooden**, **UCLA** defeats Kentucky 92-85. UCLA's **Richard Washington** is named the tournament's Most Outstanding Player.

BASKETBALL

HOCKEY

With the addition of the Washington Capitals and Kansas City Scouts, the NHL now has 18 teams that will play 80 games apiece. This year the NHL goes from a two-division league to four divisions and two conferences. Going into the quarterfinals it's the Philadelphia Flyers over the Toronto Maple Leafs, the New York Islanders over the Pittsburgh Penguins, the Buffalo Sabres over the Chicago Black Hawks, and the Montreal Canadiens over the Vancouver Canucks.

In the semifinals the Flyers take the Islanders 4-3 and the Sabres beat the Canadiens 4-2. For the Stanley Cup the Flyers beat the Sabres 4-2.

Art Ross Trophy
Phil Esposito, Bruins

Bill Masterton Memorial Trophy
Don Luce, Sabres

Calder Memorial Trophy
Eric Vail, Flames

Hart Memorial Trophy
Bobby Clarke, Flyers

Lady Byng Memorial Trophy
Marcel Dionne, Red Wings

GOLF

Masters Tournament
Jack Nicklaus

U.S. Open
Lou Graham

British Open
Tom Watson

PGA Championship
Jack Nicklaus

PGA Tour Money Leader
Jack Nicklaus
$298,149

Ryder Cup
U.S. over Britain & Ireland

LPGA Championship
Kathy Whitworth

U.S. Women's Open
Sandra Palmer

LPGA Tour Money Leader
Sandra Palmer
$76,374

British Men's Amateur
Vinny Giles

U.S. Men's Amateur
Fred Ridley

SPORTS SHORTS

AUTO RACING

Daytona 500:
Benny Parsons

Winston Cup
(NASCAR):
Richard Petty

Indianapolis 500:
Bobby Unser

Formula One
Championship:
Niki Lauda

Top Fuel NHRA
Supernationals:
Don Garlits

24 Hours of Le Mans:
**Jacky Ickx &
Derek Bell**

CYCLING

Giro d'Italia:
Fausto Bertoglio
of Italy

Tour de France:
Bernard Thévenet
of France

World Cycling
Championship:
Hennie Kuiper
of Netherlands

TENNIS

MEN'S:
Australian Open:
John Newcombe

French Open:
Björn Borg

Wimbledon:
Arthur Ashe

U.S. Open:
Manuel Orantes

WOMEN'S:
Australian Open:
Evonne Goolagong

French Open:
Chris Evert

Wimbledon:
Billie Jean King

U.S. Open:
Chris Evert

HORSE RACING

Kentucky Derby:
Foolish Pleasure

Preakness:
Master Derby

Belmont:
Avatar

BOXING

Heavyweight
Champion:
Muhammad Ali over
Joe Frazier with a
14th round TKO in
the Thrilla in Manila

FIGURE SKATING

Men's Champion:
**Sergey Nikolayevich
Volkov**
of the Soviet Union

Ladies' Champion:
Dianne de Leeuw
of the Netherlands

Pair Champions:
**Irina Rodnina &
Alexander Zaitsev**
of the Soviet Union

Ice Dancing Champion:
**Irina Moiseyeva &
Andrei Minenkov,**
of the Soviet Union

CHESS

World Chess
Championship:
American Bobby
Fischer refuses to
play and Soviet
Anatoly Karpov
gets the title.